IT AIN'T ROCKET SCIENCE !

*Revisiting the old-fashioned
approach to a successful business.*

Jeff LaFerla, OD FAAO

"If you limit your choices only
to what seems possible or
reasonable, you disconnect from
yourself what you truly want,
and all that is left is a
compromise."

Robert Fritz

Dedicated to Cassandra McKay; my friend and co-worker who inspired the title for this book.

Acknowledgments

First and foremost I wish to thank
Harry Mack Cornell, Jr. and Mike Glauber
for their 1973 decision to hire my father
into the Leggett & Platt family ... a decision
which, ultimately, made this book possible.
I thank my parents, Don and Gloria, for
teaching me about hard work, dedication
and self-confidence. To my brother, Mike,
I say thank you for your sense of humor
and for being a shining example of what
a business owner, sibling and person
should be. I'm especially grateful to my
friends Steve, Tom and Linda, whose
insights and input helped shape this book.
And finally, a very special thank you to my
sons, Peyton and Cameron, for showing me
the true meaning of unconditional love.

CONTENTS

Preface

I was blessed to grow up in the Ozarks of southwest Missouri. As a high school and college student I had the opportunity to work within the corporate headquarters of what is now a Fortune 1000 company (Leggett & Platt, Inc. / leggett.com / NYSE: LEG). That unique experience allowed for the observation, appreciation and understanding of how combining a sound business goal with the right people produces a well-oiled and results-oriented business machine.

Introduction

In today's electronic lifestyle instant access to information, data mining and managing by the numbers are the norm. Somehow, the notion of more information equals better management dictates the business mindset.

Lost in this thought process is the old-fashioned style of doing business ... a style that begins with building a dedicated team following a defined mission and continues with the development of an ongoing personal rapport with your client.

It Ain't Rocket Science ! revisits this old-fashioned approach to achieving a successful business based upon the principles of the "3 I's" in conjunction with a healthy dose of common sense and perseverance.

Chapter 1

What are the "3 I's" (and why do they matter ?)

DREAM – BELIEVE – ACHIEVE

I like to think of the "3 I's" as a game plan for how to move from the DREAM phase to the ACHIEVE phase of whatever aspirations you may have, business or otherwise.

<u>The "3 I's"</u>

INITIATE

IMPLEMENT

IMPROVE

I want to point out that the BELIEVE phase is the ultimate Catch-22 because you cannot claim to truly believe in your ability to do something unless you've taken action towards achieving it, yet you won't take the steps towards achieving that goal until you truly believe you can accomplish it. Simply put, the "3 I's" provide the tools to overcome this dilemma.

"Whatever the mind of man
can conceive and believe,
it can achieve."

Napolean Hill

Chapter 2

INITIATE

Planning

The INITIATE stage could also be called the planning stage because, whether you want to sell furniture, service computers or practice dentistry, there needs to be a time when you sit down to determine what you want to achieve and how to make it happen. Please note that the INITIATE stage is *not* a one-time event. Once you've made the decision to be a business owner, planning becomes an ongoing process that will occupy your mind any time you allow it to!

Worrying vs. Planning

Interestingly, some people confuse planning with worrying. The people that make this mistake tend to be less than optimistic on their outlook of life in general. If you are one of these folks and are considering having your own business, you may want to re-think that idea. I've paraphrased Merriam-Webster to show the distinct and exciting difference between worrying and planning:

Worrying ... mental distress from concern for something impending.

Planning ... the act of carrying out goals and procedures.

WOW ... what a stark contrast. I guess that's why investment professionals are called financial planners instead of financial worriers! The take home message here is that a thorough INITIATE stage should prevent a lot of worrying.

Common Variables

Now that we agree planning is actually a good thing, all that remains is to anticipate what variables you may encounter in designing a business plan of your own.

Common variables include:

- Sales / Marketing
- Leases / Real Estate
- Insurance
- Legal
- Personnel / Human Resources
- Inventory / Supply Chain
- Licensure / Permits
- Billing
- Accts. Payable / Receivable
- Security / Facility Management
- Information Technology
- Payroll / Benefits
- Finance / Accounting

The specifics of these, and others, depend upon the type of business you wish to start. Obtaining guidance from reputable, licensed professionals in each of the above mentioned areas is of the utmost importance.

Chapter 3

IMPLEMENT

Avoiding Paralysis by Analysis

The IMPLEMENT stage is the most difficult of the "3 I's" to put into place. Once you do begin the IMPLEMENT stage, however, you will quickly gain momentum. The goal of this stage is simply to avoid "paralysis by analysis" ... that dreaded occurrence which can stop business-owner-wanna-be's in their tracks. I think this happens when potential business owners get too caught up in the "what if's" during the INITIATE stage and simply cannot pull the trigger to get the ball rolling into the IMPLEMENT stage. Don't get me wrong, analyzing data is a good thing; it's having the ability to both analyze the data *and* develop a gut feeling about what makes sense (and why it makes sense) which separates those who conquer the IMPLEMENT stage from those who don't.

So now you're thinking "Ok, Jeff, if you're so smart then tell me what I can do to make this dreaded IMPLEMENT stage easier." Well, I'm glad you asked because I do have a few tips to help you on your way:

Follow Proven Methods

"Success is founded on a constant
state of discontentment interrupted
by brief periods of satisfaction on
the completion of a job particularly
well done."

H.M. Cornell, Jr.

WHOA! Need I say more? There's no need to reinvent the wheel, people! If nothing else from this book sticks with you, just remember that one quote and it will have a lifelong effect on how you do things.

Maintain a Positive Outlook

There is no denying the beneficial effect of a positive outlook on life. Filling your mind with thoughts of what could go right (instead of what could go wrong) allows you to keep your eyes on the goal and have confidence that you *will* achieve what you believe you *can* achieve.

Make Your Own Luck

My parents have been an amazing inspiration to me. On more than one occasion they told me "the harder you work the luckier you get" and, as usual, they were right! It's remarkable how often the tide will turn in your direction once you commit to putting in the effort required to make your dream a reality.

Avoid Feeling Overwhelmed

The large number of things to consider when beginning (and running) your own business can seem mind boggling.
Do not let this stop you! It is imperative that you find ways to keep your mind focused when your brain feels like mush. Here are a couple of my favorite tactics to combat this:

Mental Breaks ... whether it be a hobby or simply chilling out with your favorite cappuccino, allowing yourself mental breaks from time to time can give you that psychological edge required to persevere.

Compartmentalize Efforts ... wholeheartedly tackling one piece of the puzzle at a time, slowly but surely, transforms what seemed like an insurmountable obstacle into a very attainable task. Having the ability to do this, in my opinion, is the differentiating factor between those who get big things accomplished and those who don't.

Chapter 4

IMPROVE

Think Outside the Box

The IMPROVE stage brings out the detail-oriented and creative-thinking characteristics of the businessman or businesswoman. The most elusive of the "3 I's", the IMPROVE stage stems from having both common sense *and* an inherent thought process which allows you to think outside of the "normal" realm. This combination is not something that can be trained … you either have it or you don't.

Innovation

One component of this creative-thinking ability, which is useful for any of the "3 I's", is innovation. During the INITIATE stage, for instance, an innovatively structured lease agreement could literally make or break the deal. In the IMPLEMENT stage being innovative could refer to recognizing businesses in other fields utilizing strategies you could mimic to grow your own business. In a nutshell, being innovative is simply finding imaginative ways to continue guiding your efforts down the pathway of success.

Managing Minutiae, etc.

Many scenarios offer opportunities to be innovative in the IMPROVE stage. A sampling of these include:

- Managing Minutiae: seamless integration of details.

- Assessing & Implementing Technology: social media, solar panels, etc.

- Recognizing Future Potential Issues: administrative, economic, political, etc.

- Conflict Resolution: customers, employees, vendors.

Raising the Bar

The obvious goal of the IMPROVE stage is to continuously be setting the bar a little higher in order to solidify your business, in the mind of your customer, as the only game in town with respect to whatever service or product you provide.

Chapter 5

R^3

$ 1,000,000 Question

Now that we've reviewed the "3 I's", the million dollar question is this: 'How do I put together a strategy to actually make the "3 I's" happen?' Yet another good question and the answer is simple:

Have the RIGHT people

Doing the RIGHT things

For the RIGHT reasons

R^3

R-cubed

I refer to this concept as R-cubed because the results produced can have an exponentially positive impact on the success of your business. One important point to keep in mind is that R^3 may refer to an individual (you) or a team of people (employees, advisors, coaches, etc.).

R^3 Triangle

Whether starting or operating your business, R^3 refers, for example, to selection of the various professionals within the fields we discussed in chapter two of this book. Where the effectiveness of R^3 gets really exciting is when your clients' experience, through interaction with your employees, a business transaction far above and beyond their expectations.

When viewing the R^3 Triangle be sure to keep these two points in mind:

- social media reviews are crucial to the decision making process of GenX[ers] , GenY[ers], and GenZ[ers].

- human nature dictates that people like doing business with people they like.

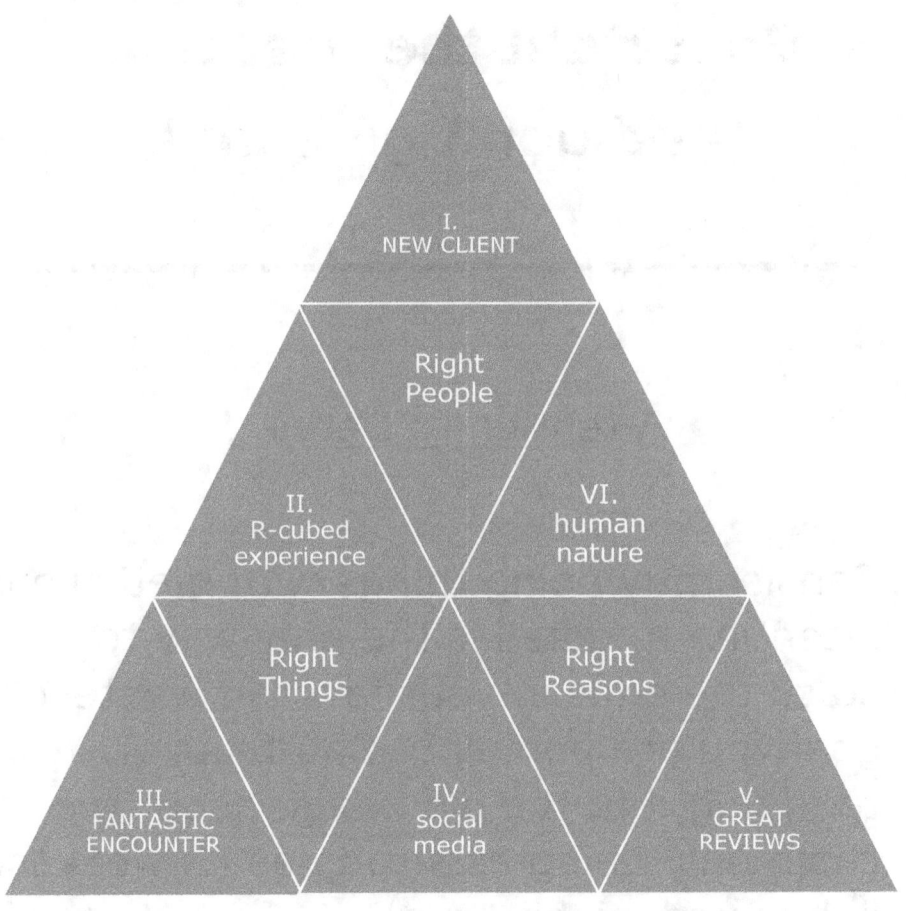

As you can see, the R³ Triangle becomes a perpetual cycle of profitable, loyal clients.

Chapter 6

Do it right the first time (and don't give up !)

Attention to Detail

Consistently doing things with meticulous attention to detail is the only way to stack the odds in your favor in whatever goal you are pursuing. Shortcuts are tempting, but the old adage about the chain only being as strong as its weakest link is undeniably true.

Contrary to what some may think, doing things the right way does not make one a control freak … instead, such actions simply reflect a deep-seated dedication to doing what it takes to achieve success.

"It is not enough that we do our best; sometimes we must do what is required."

Winston Churchill

Persistence

Of all the traits that make up us human beings, having the mental and physical fortitude to continue when you just feel like giving up is, I believe, the greatest determinant of success.

The following quote from Calvin Coolidge, 30th President of The United States of America, says it best:

Press On

"Nothing in the world can take the place of persistence. Talent will not; nothing is more common than unsuccessful men with talent. Genius will not; unrewarded genius is almost a proverb. Education alone will not; the world is full of educated derelicts. Persistence and determination alone are omnipotent."

Chapter 7

A Closing Thought

Powerful achievements don't come without significant sacrifice. In the end, only you can make the decision to realize your dreams. When faced with this dilemma don't ever forget:

"Whether you think you can,

or you think you can't

– you're right."

Henry Ford

About The Author

A Fellow of the American Academy of Optometry, Jeff LaFerla is a graduate of Missouri Southern State College and the Indiana University School of Optometry. He resides and practices in Kansas City, Missouri. A proud father and strong advocate for a healthy lifestyle, Dr. Jeff has assimilated his observations into a formula for business and personal success.

www.ingramcontent.com/pod-product-compliance
Lightning Source LLC
Chambersburg PA
CBHW071153220526
45468CB00003B/1033